"I knew that we were in trouble then. I didn't really have any misconceptions about our ability to do anything other than play music, and I was scared. [When Brian died] I thought, 'We've fuckin' had it.' "

—John Lennon, 1970

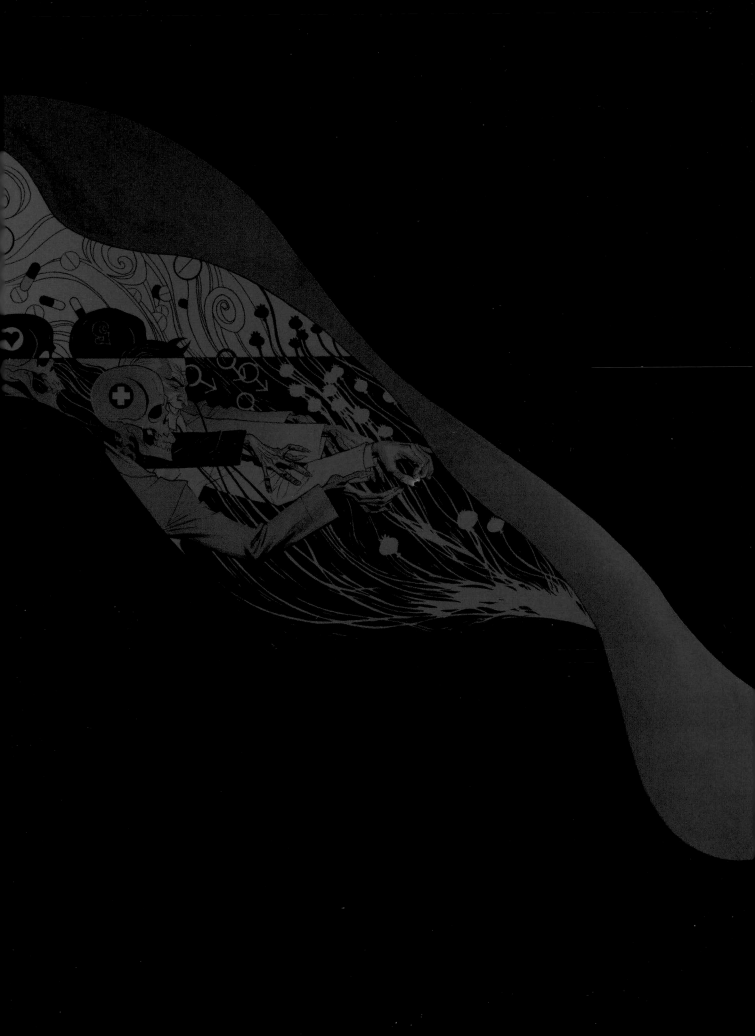

THE FIFTH
BEATLE

President and Publisher
MIKE RICHARDSON

Editor
PHILIP R. SIMON

Designer
JUSTIN A. COUCH

Digital Production and Retouch
CHRISTIANNE GOUDREAU

Special thanks to Shawna Gore, Mark Irwin,
Samantha Robertson, and Martha Thomases
for their editorial assistance and
dedication to this project.

Published by
M PRESS
A division of
Dark Horse Comics, Inc.
10956 SE Main Street
Milwaukie, OR 97222

DarkHorse.com | FifthBeatle.com | TiwaryEnt.com

3 5 7 9 10 8 6 4 2

First edition: November 2013. ISBN: 978-1-61655-256-5
Collector's Edition ISBN: 978-1-61655-265-7 | Limited Edition ISBN: 978-1-61655-257-2
To find a comics shop in your area, call the Comic Shop Locator Service toll-free at 1-888-266-4226.

WHEN I GOT A CALL FROM BRIAN, THAT'S WHEN I GREW WINGS

Introduction by Billy J. Kramer

I am baffled by the fact that Brian Epstein has not been posthumously inducted into the Rock and Roll Hall of Fame in the Non-Performer category. His name should be up in lights.

I witnessed Brian Epstein take an obscure group playing rock and roll in a cellar club called the Cavern and guide them to become the biggest music phenomenon the world has ever known. Simply put, as talented as they were, the Beatles may have never gotten out of Liverpool had it not been for Brian.

I used to see Brian in the evenings at Beatles shows in Liverpool, looking down and depressed after he had spent an entire day in London pounding the pavement, trying to secure them a record deal. But no record company wanted them. Still, he had such belief in their talents, and his enthusiasm never waned. He worked tirelessly on their behalf until he finally achieved his goal and secured the Beatles a recording deal with EMI.

Brian Epstein made the world pay attention to those four lads from Liverpool, and it saddens me that he has become a forgotten man in Beatles history.

The Fifth Beatle changes all that.

The Fifth Beatle captures Brian's love and dedication, his savvy business sense, and so many other traits that led to the Beatles' success. It finally gives Brian the credit that he so deserves. I only wish he were here to see that fifty years later, the legacy he left behind is as strong as ever, if not stronger.

Turn the page to meet Brian Epstein—my manager, mentor, and friend.

—BILLY J. KRAMER

the beatles changed our lives, brian epstein changed theirs

he made it all possible, possible for us to be having this chat today,

brian told them who they could be and helped them become it.

we were not there on that new year's day of 1962 when the beatles auditioned for decca
at their west hampstead studios.

we were not there when an a & r man, after turning down the band, chased brian out onto
the street and told him that for a hundred quid he could knock the beatles into shape for
another audition.

the humiliation, the pain . . . brian already had at least two social marks against him—
he was jewish and gay.

christ, you know it ain't easy. dusty springfield was catholic and gay but she was able to sing
her way through it.

brian had to stand in the wings and watch his lads twist and shout

but those wings became the wings of the world

from scunthorpe to shea stadium in three super fast, incredible singalong years the world was
given a songbook it has never stopped singing and an idea as to what a life could be about.

brian persevered against all odds and got his lads a recording contract and that act changed
all our lives for the better.

if brian had loved himself as much as he loved the beatles he may have still been with us today,

but we do have all that they did together . . .

andrew loog oldham
bogotá, mm13

DEDICATIONS

VIVEK J. TIWARY

for
Nandini Beharry Tiwary
and
Malka "Queenie" Epstein

ANDREW C. ROBINSON

for
Jim and Leah

Part I: Or I'll Dress You in Mourning

1961...

WONDROUS PLACE.

A SPOT IN A STORM...

...TO CUDDLE UP...

...AND STAY NICE AND WARM.

HER SOFT EMBRACE...

...LIKE SATIN AND LACE.

WONDROUS PLACE.

MORNING, MR. BRIAN! I'VE TEA STEEPING ON YOUR DESK.

YOU'RE A GIFT, MOXIE.

BRIAN. HOW ARE YOU?

RECORDS ARE SELLING RELIABLY, DADDY.

I'M ASKING ABOUT YOU, NOT OUR RECORD STORE!

STEADY SUCCESS. AND THUS...RATHER DULL.

I'M LOOKING FOR A RECORD I CAN'T FIND ANYWHERE. THE BEATLES' "MY BONNIE."

GOOD CHOICE-- THE BEATS ARE FAB!

YOU STUMBLED HOME LATE AGAIN LAST NIGHT, AND YOU LOOK HURT. I'M JUST WORRIED--

EXCUSE ME, DADDY.

MR. BRIAN, WE DON'T SEEM TO HAVE THE BEATLES' RECORD.

WE MUST. POPULAR LOCAL BAND.

THE RECORD'S BY TONY SHERIDAN, REALLY. THE BEATS ARE BACKING HIM.

AND IT'S ON A GERMAN LABEL, RIGHT? I THINK THEY'RE CALLED "THE BEAT BROTHERS" ON THE RECORD.

"THE BEAT BROTHERS" ...?

BUT IT'S *THEM* I LIKE-- THE BEATLES ARE *GORGEOUS!*

WELL. IT IS A STRICT STORE POLICY THAT WE WILL LOCATE *ANY* RECORD FOR *ANY* CUSTOMER. MOXIE, PLEASE PUT "MY BONNIE" ON ORDER.

THANK GOD.

INDEED? WHY DO YOU SAY?

YOU'VE NEVER SEEN THE BEATLES?! THEY'RE THE BEST GROUP LIVERPOOL'S GOT--AND THEY'RE ALWAYS AT THE CAVERN ROUND THE CORNER!

WELL, THE CAVERN ISN'T THE SORT OF CLUB I TYPICALLY FREQUENT...THOUGH I AM INTRIGUED. DO YOU THINK YOU COULD HELP ME GET IN? MAKE THE NECESSARY ARRANGEMENTS?

WHEN WOULD YOU LIKE?

...BEFORE HIS FIRST DANCE WITH THE VALIANT BULLS OF SPAIN.

"TONIGHT I'LL BUY YOU A HOUSE...

WITH MY HELP, THE BEATLES COULD BE INTERNATIONAL STARS.

INTERNATIONAL. AND I THOUGHT I WAS THE VISIONARY.

THOUGH REGARDING CONCERTS, I AM CONFIDENT I CAN IMMEDIATELY SECURE BETTER FEES AND MORE FREQUENT ENGAGEMENTS.

WELL, THEN-- PERHAPS IT'S TIME TO GET ENGAGED AFTER ALL!

TIME? IT WOULD APPEAR THAT BEATLES HAVE A POOR CONCEPT OF TIME.

YOU'RE LATE.

NO, I'M NOT--I'M GEORGE.

SEE? A BEATLE DOESN'T MISS A BEAT.

THEN WHERE IS PAUL?

I'VE JUST BEEN ROUND HIS HOUSE. HE'S IN THE BATH.

THEN HE'S GOING TO BE EXTREMELY LATE!

BUT VERY CLEAN.

WELL IF YOU AIM FOR SUCCESS, YOU'LL NEED TO BE BOTH CLEAN AND PUNCTUAL!

RIGHT, WHAT DID I MISS?

YOU'RE VERY LATE.

NO, I'M NOT--I'M PAUL.

21

 MR. EPSTEIN'S AN ASTRONOMER AND A ROMANTIC--HE'S SEEING STARS, AND HE'S OFFERED ME HIS HAND.

 A HANDS-ON MARRIAGE? SPEAK THEN, OR FOREVER HOLD YOUR PEACE.

 WELL. NOW THAT YOU'RE *ALL* HERE!

 WHILE I DO NOT HAVE PRIOR EXPERIENCE IN THE MANAGEMENT OF ARTISTES, I'M CERTAIN I CAN IMMEDIATELY RAISE YOUR COMPENSATION AT THE CAVERN CLUB FROM 7 POUNDS, 10 SHILLINGS, TO 14 OR 15 POUNDS.

BUT THIS IS SMALL THINKING. I WOULD LIKE TO HELP YOU CREATE A *LOOK*, AN IMAGE THAT WILL BRING YOU MORE FANS AND MORE ATTENTION.

 I BELIEVE EACH OF YOU ALREADY HAS SOMETHING INDIVIDUAL...

 WHICH COULD BE HIGHLY COMMERCIAL...

 ...IF YOU HAVE SOMEONE TO PUSH IT TO THE TOP.

 SO WITH MY HELP, I BELIEVE YOU WILL BECOME IMPORTANT, INTERNATIONAL STARS!

 RIGHT, THEN. WHERE'S THE CONTRACT? I'LL SIGN IT.

 MONUMENTAL ?

 TO BATHE AND TO BE BOLD, IN RICHNESS AND IN WEALTH, 'TIL DEATH DO US PART. I DO.

 HOLD A MOMENT-- WE'VE HAD BLOKES LOOKING AFTER OUR AFFAIRS BEFORE.

INDEED. YOUR FORMER AGENT TOLD ME NOT TO TOUCH YOU WITH A F--WITH A BARGE POLE.

YET I WILL PROMISE YOU A CONTRACT WITH A PROMINENT RECORD COMPANY.

A RECORD CONTRACT?!?!?!

IT SHOULD NOT BE DIFFICULT. NEMS IS ONE OF THE MOST SUCCESSFUL BRITISH RECORD RETAILERS. I HAVE STRONG RELATIONS AT ALL THE RECORD COMPANIES.

BUT WHY? YOU WERE TOLD NOT TO TOUCH US WITH A FUCKING BARGE POLE!

WELL...WHY DO YOU WRITE MUSIC?

WELL...BECAUSE WE HAVE TO, I RECKON. WE HAVEN'T GOT A CHOICE, REALLY.

EXACTLY. AND THAT'S WHY I WANT TO MANAGE YOU AS WELL.

LOOK, IT ISN'T ABOUT MONEY. I MEAN, I TRULY THINK YOU COULD BE INTERNATIONAL STARS-- EVEN MORE THAN THAT! BUT IT ISN'T JUST SUCCESS.

WHEN I FIRST SAW YOU AT THE CAVERN-- IT'S WHAT I SAW, HOW I FELT.

A PART OF SOMETHING SPECIAL, SOMETHING IMPORTANT...

...AND THAT I SIMPLY HAVEN'T A CHOICE.

RIGHT, THEN. WHERE'S THE CONTRACT? I'LL SIGN IT.

23

REX MAKIN CAME BY EARLIER-- HE SAYS BRIAN'S BEEN FOR SOME LEGAL ADVICE ABOUT THAT POP GROUP HE'S TOLD US ABOUT. BRIAN'S TAKING IT VERY SERIOUSLY...

MR. MAKIN CERTAINLY DOESN'T THINK SO. CALLS IT ANOTHER ONE OF "BRIAN EPSTEIN'S FOOLISH PHASES."

MR. MAKIN TOLD ME HE'S GOT TICKETS FOR THE FOOTIE AGAINST EVERTON! AND SHANKS IS CHANGING THE TEAM STRIP TO ALL RED.

WELL IS IT?

SHANKS SAYS, "IF EVERTON WERE PLAYING AT THE BOTTOM OF THE GARDEN, I'D PULL THE CURTAINS!"

THE BEATLES ARE NOT JUST A POP GROUP.

THEY'RE NOT?

DADDY, THE BEATLES COULD PUT LIVERPOOL ON THE *WORLD* MAP--MUCH MORE THAN ANY FOOTBALL CLUB COULD!

THEY NEED ME. WITH MY HELP, THE BEATLES ARE GOING TO BE BIGGER... THAN *ELVIS!*

THAT'S AWFULLY BIG.

NOT NEARLY BIG ENOUGH!

BRIAN. YOUR FATHER AND I, WE LOVE YOU VERY MUCH. YOU KNOW WE'VE ALWAYS SUPPORTED YOUR VARIOUS PURSUITS--THE ARMY, DRAMA SCHOOL...

DRESSMAKING.

FASHION DESIGNING!

SO WE STAND FIRMLY BY YOU.

INDEED. WE WANT YOU TO BE HAPPY. BUT THERE IS STILL THE ISSUE OF OUR STORE--

I'M NOT LEAVING THE STORE! I WILL MAINTAIN MY RESPONSIBILITIES WITH THE STORE *AND* THE FAMILY.

YES, BUT HAVE YOU THOUGHT THAT THROUGH? HOW YOU'RE GOING TO DO IT ALL?

I WON'T LET THE FAMILY DOWN! I CAN DO IT!

I'M NOT ASKING *IF*--I'M ASKING YOU *HOW.*

BRIAN! YOU'RE SMART AND HANDSOME. YOU HAVE SOME MEANS AND RUN A SUCCESSFUL BUSINESS.

I'LL FIND A WAY.

WE ARE ALREADY VERY PROUD OF YOU.

INDEED, BRIAN. GOOD LUCK WITH THE GROUP.

BIGGER THAN ELVIS?

BIGGER THAN ELVIS!!!

ARE WE LATE?

JOHN'S WEARING A SUIT.

SUITS HIM NICELY.

YOU'RE ALL GETTING ONE.

HE'S SERIOUS.

SUIT YOURSELF.

CYNTHIA WILL LOVE THIS.

AND AFTER SUITS, MATCHING HAIRCUTS. DECENT ONES.

AND NO MORE SMOKING, DRINKING, OR SWEARING ONSTAGE!

YOU CAN'T BE F--

THOUGH DESPITE THESE SUITS, IT'S ESSENTIAL THAT WE'RE FROM LIVERPOOL. AND WORKING CLASS, AT THAT.

LIVERPOOL, LA?

HOW MUCH ARE THOSE MOONDOGGIES IN THE WINDOW?!

I RATHER FANCY LOOKING FANCY.

ARE YOU SERIOUS ABOUT THE HAIRCUTS? AND THE CUSSING?

WE CAN'T AFFORD SUITS!

OR HAIRCUTS.

WE CAN. THEY'RE ON ME.

NO, I THINK THEY'RE ON US.

THANKS, EPPY. THIS IS ALL VERY GENEROUS. BUT HOW WILL WE EXPLAIN 'EM?

ALL YOU HAVE TO DO IS ACT NATURALLY--NO STRAIGHT ANSWERS! MAKE A RIDDLE, WRITE A SONG. LIKE YOU'RE TALKING TO ME NOW.

IT'S ONE OF THE THINGS I LOVE ABOUT YOU.

"FOUR LADS FROM LIVERPOOL."

THAT'S SOMETHING THE WHOLE WORLD CAN EMBRACE--

THE WORLD?

EMBRACING HOME WILL PROVE THE BEST WAY TO LEAVE IT! THAT, SUITS, AND HAIRCUTS...

DON'T WORRY ABOUT THE BUSINESS. PLAY YOUR INSTRUMENTS, AND I WILL PLAY THE BUSINESS AS MY INSTRUMENT. ONLY YOU'LL NEVER HAVE TO HEAR IT.

IF I DON'T HEAR IT, I WON'T APPRECIATE YOU.

WELL YOU ALREADY DON'T APPRECIATE ME, SO AT LEAST THIS WILL GIVE YOU A SMART REASON NOT TO.

THEN WE SUBMIT, DEFENSELESS BEFORE YOUR STRATEGICONFIDENCE.

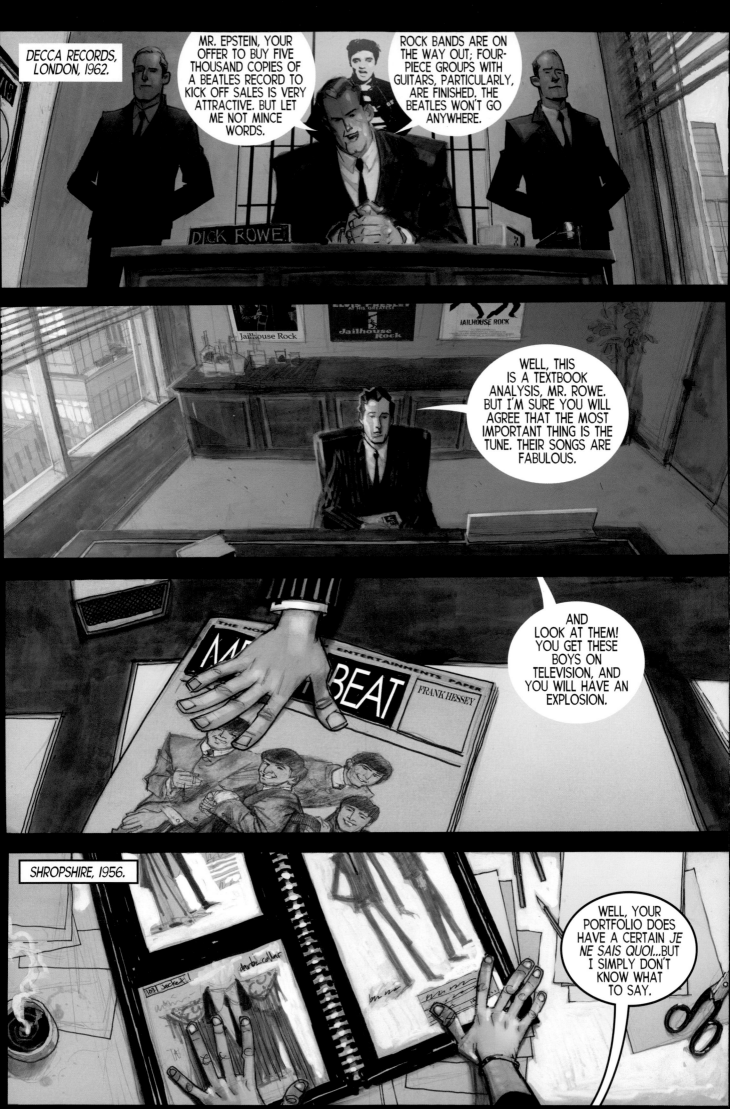

...WOULD BE TO JUST GET SOME REST.

Epstein, Brian

THESE SHOULD HELP WITH YOUR EXHAUSTION. AND CONSISTENT USE OVER TIME WILL ALSO HELP DEAL WITH YOUR OTHER... PROBLEM.

DOCTOR?

THE INTIMATE... INCLINATIONS.

AH. THANK YOU, DOCTOR.

PLEASURE. JUST MAKE SURE YOU DON'T MIX THEM WITH ANYTHING ELSE...AND REMEMBER...

...YOU CAN NEVER HAVE ENOUGH FLOWERS!

WE'VE RECEIVED ANOTHER REJECTION. EMI RECORDS: "THE PUBLIC WILL BE CONFUSED BY A BAND WITH TWO LEAD SINGERS."

BOLLOCKS THEY WILL!

ALL FOUR OF EMI'S A&R MEN HAVE PASSED.

NO. ONLY THREE.

THE FOURTH, GEORGE MARTIN, WAS ON VACATION WHEN EMI REVIEWED THE DEMONSTRATION RECORD. HE DOESN'T KNOW...AND HE'S AGREED TO SEE ME.

BRILLIANT!

EVERY LABEL HAS PASSED. DECCA, COLUMBIA, PYE...EVEN PHILIPS AND ORIOLE.

SO IT'S PARAMOUNT TO MEET MR. MARTIN BEFORE HE REALIZES HIS COMPANY HAS ALREADY REJECTED OUR BEATLES. HE RUNS PARLOPHONE.

DON'T THEY MAKE--

COMEDY RECORDS, YES.

MILLIGAN, THOUGH! AND SOME FINE CLASSICAL RECORDS AS WELL.

THESE BOYS WILL BE BIGGER THAN ELVIS--EVEN IF IT'S ON MR. MARTIN'S ILL-SUITED COMEDY LABEL.

I WILL *PROVE* IT...AND I'VE PROMISED THE BOYS A RECORD DEAL.

SO PLEASE MAKE THE NECESSARY ARRANGEMENTS FOR ANOTHER TRIP TO LONDON! IMMEDIATELY.

ONE SWEET DREAM.

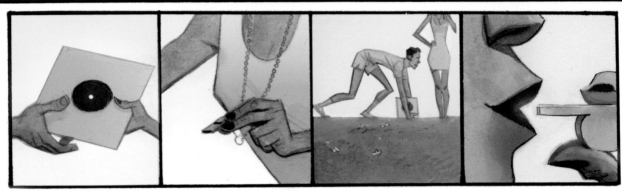

THAT'S WHAT I WANT.

34

"TELEGRAM THE BEATLES IN HAMBURG--CONGRATULATIONS, BOYS!!

"EMI REQUESTS RECORDING SESSION.

"PLEASE REHEARSE NEW MATERIAL!"

JOHN! WHAT ARE YOU DOING HERE? YOU BELONG AT A BEATLES ENGAGEMENT IN TAUNTON!

WELL. I'VE DONE BOOKED MESELF A DIFFERENT ENGAGEMENT. CALL IT A SURPRISE GIG. CYN'S PREGGIE.

CYNTHIA. IS. PREGNANT.

JOHN WINSTON LENNON, YOU AIN'T NOTHIN' BUT A HOUND DOG. SO BEING A GOOD DOG, JOHN MOUNTS HIS FAITHFUL BITCH--THAT'S PROPER FOR FEMALE DOG, YOU KNOW--AND, WELL, OUTCOME: THE PUPS.

EPPY, WHATEVER AM I GOING TO DO? I ADORE CYN, BUT I DON'T KNOW HOW TO HANDLE THIS.

YOU MUST MARRY HER IMMEDIATELY.

I THOUGHT YOU SAID BEATLES OUGHT NEVER BE MARRIED.

THEY OUGHT NOT, BUT THEY WILL. AND THEY OUGHT TO BE DECENT LADS ABOVE ALL ELSE.

CYN IS A GOOD GIRL. SHE'LL MAKE A FINE WIFE.

I WILL PAY FOR THE WEDDING. MOXIE-- NO. I'LL MAKE ALL THE NECESSARY ARRANGEMENTS MYSELF, PERSONALLY...

AND YOU MUST HAVE A SUITABLE HOME WITH ENOUGH ROOM AND LIGHT TO RAISE A HAPPY CHILD...SO YOU WILL HAVE MY FLAT ON FALKNER STREET. I'LL TAKE CARE OF EVERYTHING.

BUT WE MUST NOT LET THE PRESS FIND OUT. IT WOULD BE VERY BAD FOR YOUR IMAGE. AND YOU MUST RESUME TOUR STRAIGHTAWAY.

YEAH. BEATLES OUGHT NEVER BE MARRIED.

JOHN. IT'S A LOVELY, LUCKY THING TO HAVE CHILDREN.

MOXIE, PLEASE ORDER TEN THOUSAND COPIES OF "LOVE ME DO" FOR NEMS.

WE'VE--

DO *NOT* QUESTION MY JUDGMENT! AND DO *NOT* CHECK WITH DADDY OR CLIVE FIRST, OR *I'LL HAVE YOUR POSITION!* THEY WILL SELL!!

LOVE ME DO
(Lennon—McCartney)
·THE BEATLES·

WE'VE ALSO RECEIVED A CONTRACT FROM A STRANGE COMPANY ABOUT MAKING BEATLES...DOLLS.

MOXIE...BE A BIT TOLERANT OF ME AT MY WORST. REALLY, I DON'T LIKE, OR WANT, TO HURT ANYBODY.

NOW-- WHAT WAS IT?

UMMM... BEATLES DOLLS?

AH, YES. DOLLS, WIGS, LUNCHBOXES. I WANT THE BEATLES TO HAVE MERCHANDISE BEFORE WE ATTACK AMERICA.

MERCHANDISE? DOLLS? ATTACK AMERICA? I'M SORRY, MR. BRIAN, I DON'T UNDERSTAND!

MOXIE...WHY DO YOU PUT UP WITH THIS?

PARDON?

ALL THIS CAN'T BE EASY FOR YOU.

THERE ARE THE BEATLES. AND YOU'RE INVALUABLE TO ME.

BUT THERE MUST BE EASIER POSITIONS.

WELL, YES...BUT THERE'S ONLY ONE BRIAN EPSTEIN.

MOXIE, I--

"LOVE ME DO" HAS REACHED NUMBER 17.

THEN PLEASE. PLEASE. ME.

HE LOOKS A LITTLE LIKE JOHN. HE'S GORGEOUS.

JOHN--*WE*-- WOULD LIKE YOU TO BE JULIAN'S GODFATHER.

GODFATHER? IN MY WHOLE LIFE, I'VE NEVER...I'M SO HONORED.

HE WILL NEVER WANT, AS LONG AS I LIVE.

...THAT IF THE LIVER BIRDS WERE EVER TO FLY AWAY...

...LIVERPOOL WOULD SINK INTO THE SEA.

A MYTHICAL LOST CITY...

...WASHED AWAY BY TIME AND RAIN.

WONDROUS PLACE.

Spain...

1963.

WE'VE REALLY DONE IT NOW.

WHAT'S THAT?

MADE IT--TO THE "TOPPERMOST OF THE POPPERMOST."

HOW DO YOU MEAN?

HMPH. HARDLY.

ENGLAND'S A STEP. BUT AMERICA. THAT'S THE GATEWAY TO THE WORLD.

DON'T BE DAFT.

DON'T BE SOFT.

HE UPLIFTS THE ARENA, THE CITY, THE NATION. VERY BEAUTIFUL.

SO YES, I DO FIND HIM ATTRACTIVE, BUT NOT IN THE WAY YOU MIGHT THINK.

AND HIM?

NOT SO MUCH.

YOU'RE MAD. HE'S GOT ALL THE BIRDS!

WOMEN AREN'T NATURALLY THE BEST ARBITERS OF TASTE. HE'S QUITE ORDINARY.

AND THAT ONE?

NO.

YES.

WELL.

IT'S TOO BAD I'M NOT QUEER.

NEW YORK CITY, 1963.

WE LIKE YOUR BOYS, MR. EPSTEIN, AND I'LL BE HONEST THAT I'M IMPRESSED WITH YOUR ENTHUSIASM.

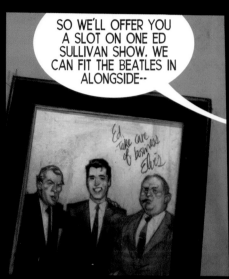

SO WE'LL OFFER YOU A SLOT ON ONE ED SULLIVAN SHOW. WE CAN FIT THE BEATLES IN ALONGSIDE--

--MR. K. THE AKROBAT AND HENRY THE DANCING HORSE.

MR. SULLIVAN, I APPLAUD YOU FOR RECOGNIZING THE VALUE OF PROVIDING THE BEATLES WITH THEIR FIRST AMERICAN EXPOSURE, BUT--

≈AH-HEM!≈

≈SIGH≈

BUT MY BOYS MUST *HEADLINE.*

WELL, MY HANDS ARE TIED, MR. EPSTEIN, AS I CAN'T DO ANYTHING WITHOUT CHECKING WITH MR. SULLIVAN--AND THAT COULD TAKE AWHILE. SO I STRONGLY SUGGEST YOU TAKE THE CURRENT OFFER.

AND LET ME PUT THIS AS GRACEFULLY AS I CAN. WE THINK THE BEATLES ARE NOTHING MORE THAN A--

--NOVELTY ACT.

THE BEATLES HAVE PERFORMED FOR THE QUEEN OF ENGLAND!!

EXACTLY MY POINT. THE BEATLES ARE NO ELVIS...AND WITH RESPECT, YOU'RE NO COLONEL PARKER.

WELL, PLEASE TELL *MR. SULLIVAN*--THAT WE'D BE PLEASED TO BE ON HIS SHOW BECAUSE HE IS THE BEST.

BUT THE BEATLES ALSO ARE THE BEST, AND SO I WILL NOT HAVE THEM IN ANY CAPACITY OTHER THAN HEADLINING.

I'LL RELAY THE MESSAGE WHEN I CAN, BUT I'M SURE MR. SULLIVAN *WON'T* HAVE THEM HEADLINE. NOT ONE SINGLE SHOW.

WE WANT YOUR BOYS, MR. EPSTEIN--BUT REMEMBER, THE BEATLES ARE UNKNOWN HERE IN THE US.

WELL. IF MR. SULLIVAN WON'T HAVE US HEADLINE ONE SINGLE SHOW, TELL HIM WE WILL AGREE TO HEADLINE *THREE* SHOWS INSTEAD...

...FOR HALF OF WHAT YOU'D PAY US FOR ONE PERFORMANCE.

THIS TRIP WILL COST AT LEAST FIFTY THOUSAND! WHO'LL COVER THAT? CBS WON'T.

I WILL. PERSONALLY.

LET ME GET THIS STRAIGHT. YOU PROPOSE WE PAY YOU HALF OF ONE PERFORMANCE--FOR THREE PERFORMANCES?

HEADLINING. AND IF THINGS GO WELL, I'D LIKE TO DISCUSS ANOTHER ARTISTE I'VE JUST SIGNED--A LOVELY SONGBIRD NAMED CILLA BLACK.

WHATEVER.

I'M CERTAIN SHE'S GOING TO BE A BIG TELEVISION PERSONALITY--

WELL, I'LL HAVE TO CHECK WITH MR. SULLIVAN.

YOU'VE GOT A DEAL!

THE BEATLES WILL HEADLINE THE ED SULLIVAN SHOW!

55

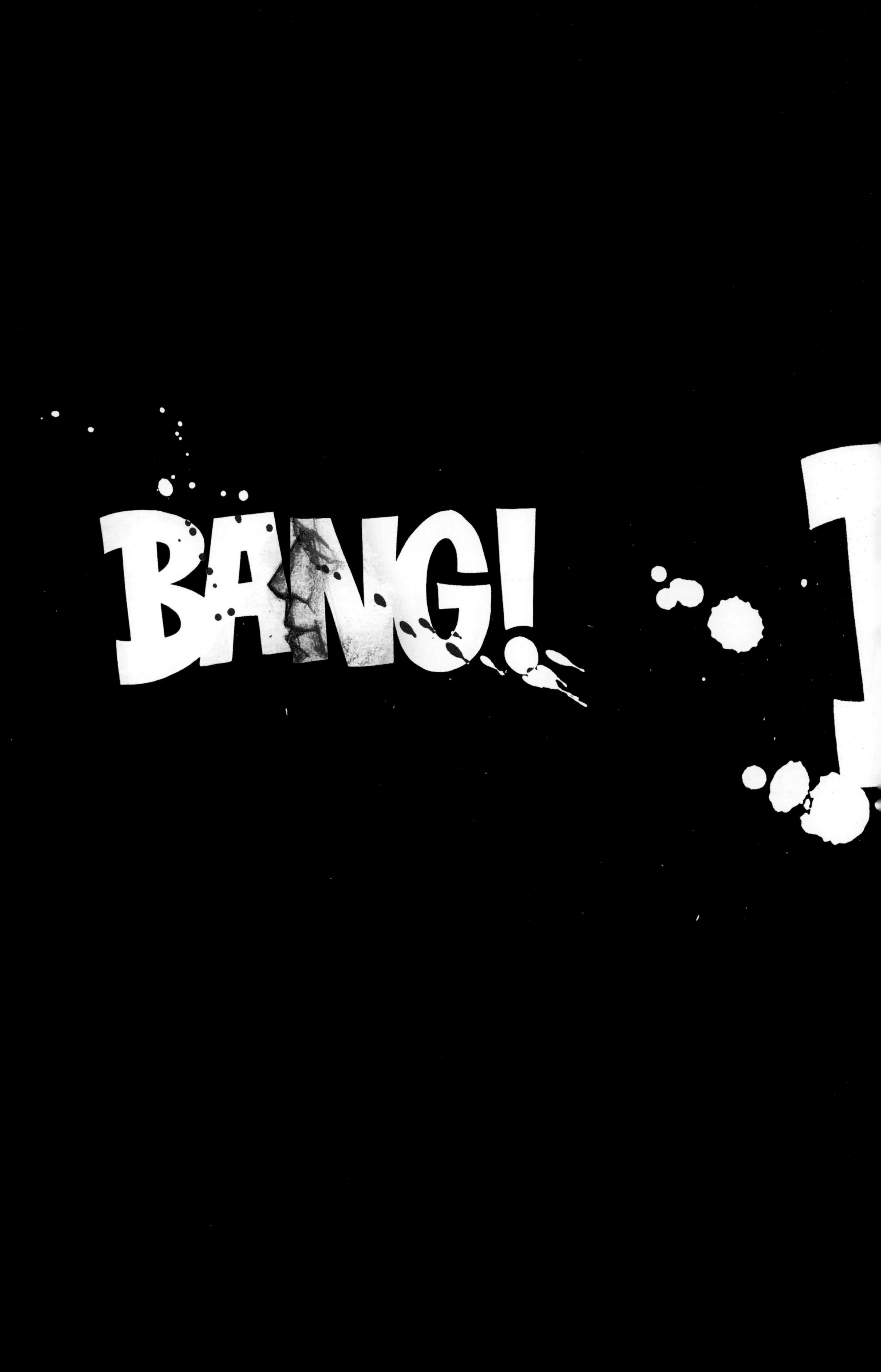
BANG!

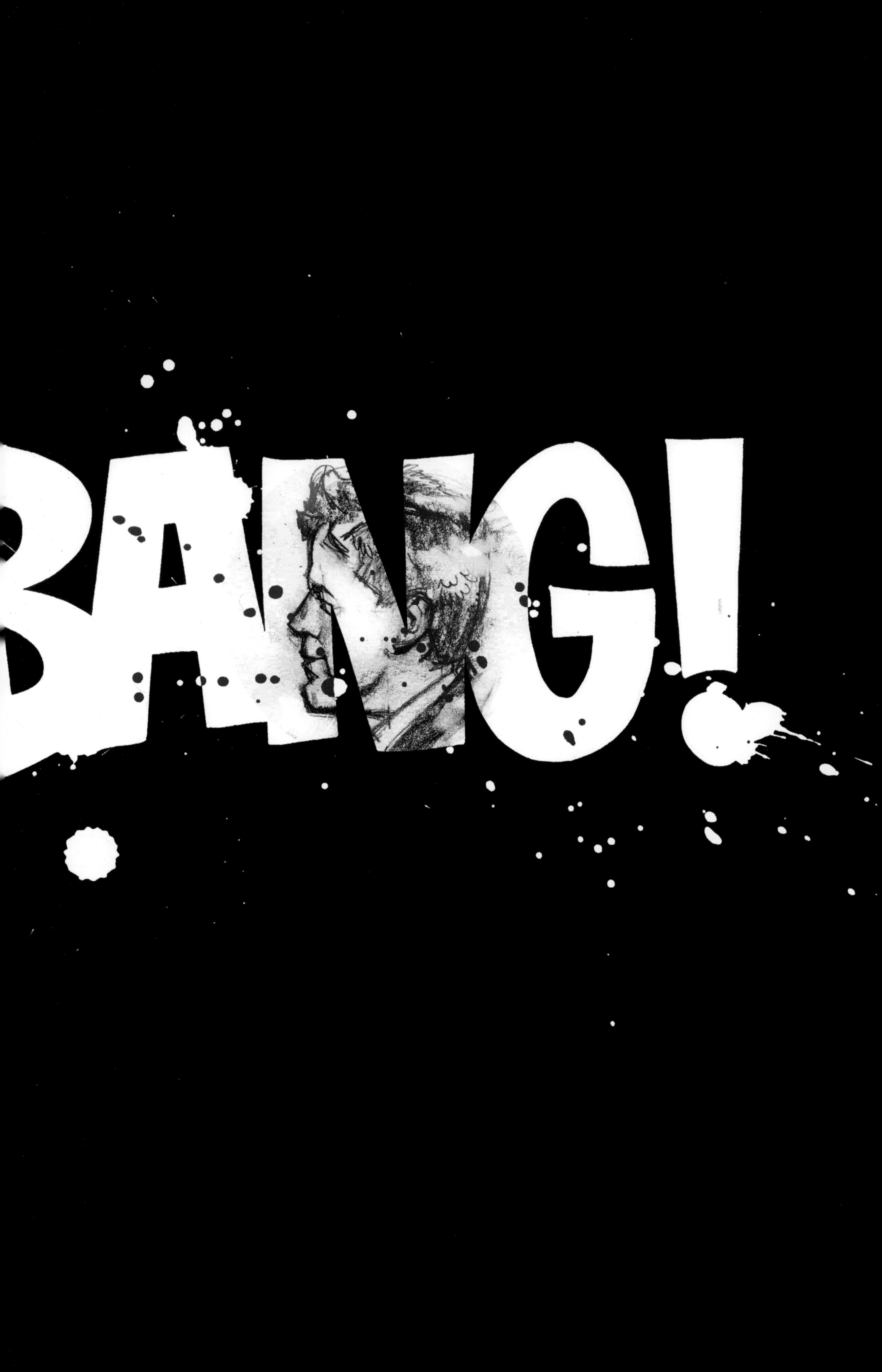
BANG!

I KNOW, MUMMY, EVERYONE IN LONDON IS SHOCKED AS WELL. I CAN'T IMAGINE WHAT IT'S LIKE IN AMERICA. THEY SAY THIS JOHNSON PERSON REPLACES PRESIDENT KENNEDY STRAIGHTAWAY...

I *WAS* JUST THERE, BUT NEW YORK IS THOUSANDS OF KILOMETERS FROM TEXAS.

DON'T CRY, MUMMY, I'M FINE. YOU'RE FINE...I'LL CALL AGAIN TOMORROW. LOVE TO DADDY AND CLIVE... BYE NOW.

Click.

"As a bullfighter you're completely alone, even if thousands of people are watching your fight. It is an unimaginable loneliness. The only thing you can sense at that moment is the bull."
—The great matador Juan Belmonte

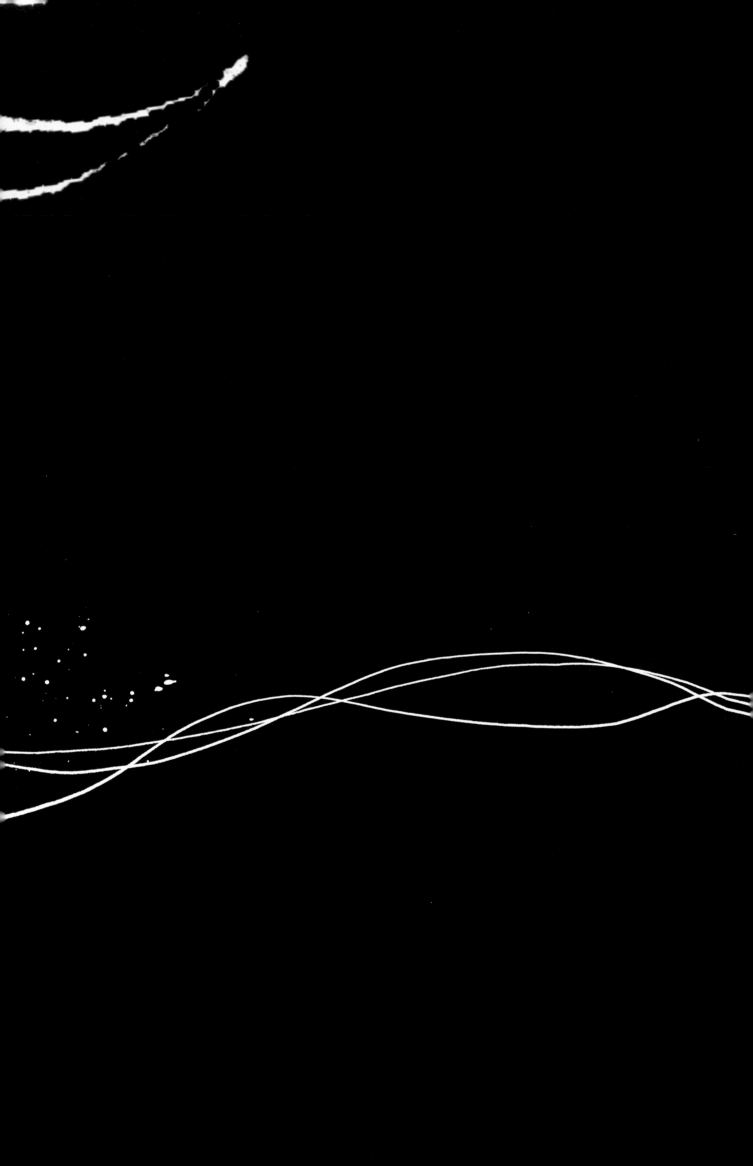

"A MAN WHO HATED BIGOTRY..."

"WHO BELIEVED THAT ALL MEN WERE EQUAL IN THE SIGHT OF GOD..."

MOXIE! WHAT'S WRONG WITH YOU?! HAVE YOU NO SENSE OF PRIVACY?!

"TOLERANT AND HUMAN."

I'M SORRY, MR. BRIAN! I JUST WANTED TO SHOW YOU THESE AS SOON AS THEY ARRIVED.

COME, IT'S ALL RIGHT...YOU KNOW HOW I CAN GET.

THAT WAS A SPECIAL ANNOUNCEMENT FROM PRIME MINISTER ALEC DOUGLAS-HOME...

ARE YOU NOT FEELING WELL, MR. BRIAN? IS THERE ANYTHING I CAN DO?

NO, IT'S NOTHING LIKE THAT! I'M FINE.

A BIT LONELY, PERHAPS... BUT FINE!

WELL, HOW ARE YOU GOING TO HANDLE YOUR LONELINESS BY STAYING ALONE?

WELL...WILL WHATEVER'S IN THAT BAG KEEP ME WARM AT NIGHT?

HA! I SUPPOSE THEY COULD DO.

GOOD LORD! WHERE DID YOU GET THOSE?

YOU SIGNED A RUSH DEAL FOR THEM! YOU SAID THE TIMING WAS CRITICAL.

YES--BUT I THOUGHT I'D HAVE SOME APPROVAL BEFORE THEY WERE MADE. THEY DON'T LOOK ANYTHING LIKE I'D HOPED!

BUT THE BEATLES HAVE DOLLS! THEY'RE BRILLIANT. AND CUTE, TOO!

I'M LUCY, AND I'M CALLING TO REQUEST "I WANNA HOLD YOUR HAND" BY THE BEATLES!

UH-HUH, I CALLED BEFORE, 'CUZ I LOVE THEM!

I'M TEN! THANKS!

HAPPY NEW YEAR AND GOD BLESS AMERICA!

MOXIE, PLEASE MAKE THE NECESSARY ARRANGEMENTS FOR OUR TRIP TO AMERICA. THE TIMING IS PERFECT.

BESIDES, EPPY SAYS THE TIMING IS PERFECT.

SO IF HE SAYS IT, IT MUST BE SO.

BLUE SKIES SMILING AT ME...
DAD, I DIDN'T CALL TO ARGUE ABOUT POLITICS.
AMERICAN
PAN AM
I'M CALLING TO SAY I'M FINE! I'M IN NEW YORK CITY. I HITCHED. GOING TO IDLEWILD...

AMERICA, 1964.

NEW YORK CITY, 1965.

MR. BRIAN? YOUR MEETING WITH MR. NAT WEISS-- LARRY PARNES'S REFERRAL.

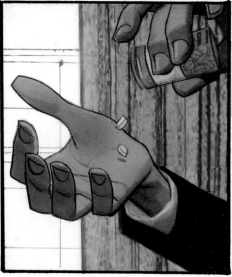

MR. WEISS. HAVE YOU READ MY AUTOBIOGRAPHY, A CELLARFUL OF NOISE?

NO, I'M SORRY. I HAVEN'T.

WELL. I'M HAPPY TO HEAR THAT. BECAUSE YOU CAN'T BELIEVE EVERYTHING YOU READ. ESPECIALLY WHEN IT COMES TO MYSELF AND THE BEATLES.

MYTHOLOGY IS BETTER AND MORE FONDLY REMEMBERED THAN HISTORY. IT'S MORE ENTERTAINING! SO WE CREATE LEGENDS RATHER THAN RECOUNT TRUTHS-- WOULDN'T YOU AGREE?

PLEASE CALL ME NAT. IS THERE SOMETHING SPECIFIC I CAN ADVISE YOU ON?

THE BEATLES AND I ARE QUITE WEALTHY MEN.

WELL, I PREFER TO KNOW WHAT ACTUALLY HAPPENED THAN FANTASIES THAT DIDN'T.

I'M HAPPY TO HEAR THAT, TOO! A GOOD QUALITY FOR AN ATTORNEY, MR. WEISS.

I HAVEN'T TOLD ANYONE THIS, BUT I'M TERRIBLY ASHAMED.

LOOK, I'M SURE EVEN COLONEL PARKER HAS HAD LEGAL PROBLEMS WITH ELVIS.

AND IT'S STANDARD FOR ARTISTS TO BEAR THE EXPENSES OF THEIR MANAGER RENEGOTIATING DEALS AFTER THEY'VE ACQUIRED STATURE AS LEVERAGE...

BRIAN. I'VE SAID IT BEFORE-- YOU GOTTA TELL THE BEATLES ABOUT THESE DEALS. THERE'S NOTHING TO BE ASHAMED OF! YOU HAVEN'T *LOST* THEM MONEY.

YOU'VE DONE AN INCREDIBLE JOB IN ALMOST EVERY WAY. NO ONE CAN DENY THAT!

WITH THE BEATLES THERE ARE NO STANDARDS-- AND THERE HAVE BEEN NO FAILURES.

AT LEAST, THAT'S THE MYTH... ONE I'D LIKE TO PERPETUATE.

WELL THE TRUTH ALWAYS GETS OUTED, EVENTUALLY.

ONLY WHEN IT BECOMES MORE SENSATIONAL THAN THE MYTH.

THEN LET'S GIVE THE TRUTH A REST AND HAVE SOME FUN. I WANT TO TAKE YOU TO KELLY'S--GIVE YOU SOMETHING TO BE TRULY ASHAMED OF.

I DIDN'T KNOW PLACES LIKE THIS EXIST!
THEY DON'T, BRIAN--IT'S A MYTH!
NOT EVEN IN SPAIN! HAVE YOU BEEN? I'VE GOT A BIT OF THE MATADOR IN ME MYSELF.
IS THAT RIGHT? DO TELL...
SPAIN! FROM THE US TO LONDON VIA SPAIN. WHAT DON'T YOU UNDERSTAND?
YOU'VE CARRIED ME TO KELLY'S, I'LL CARRY YOU TO THE CORRIDAS!
I'M AFRAID TO ASK YOU TO KEEP TALKING!
SPAIN AND THE CORRIDAS! THE BULLFIGHT, NAT! IT'S WILD, PASSIONATE, DANGEROUS!
AND THE BOYS!
NOW WHAT ABOUT THAT ONE?
WELL WHO DO YOU THINK YOU ARE, BRIAN EPSTEIN?
WHY? DO YOU KNOW HIM?

KNOW THE TYPE--A GARDEN-VARIETY HUSTLER. YOU'RE WORRIED ABOUT REPUTATION? STAY AWAY FROM THAT.
TRUTH!
WELL, I'VE BEEN SURPRISING PEOPLE MY ENTIRE LIFE...
LET'S TASTE THE FRUITS OF YOUR "BRAVE NEW WORLD."
MY FRIENDS CALL ME DIZZ.
AND MY FRIENDS CALL ME "EL BRIANO"!

LONDON.

POP POP POP POP POP POP

POP POP POP POP POP

HONESTLY, THERE'S NO ONE ELSE I'D RATHER BE WITH.

REALLY? NO ONE AT ALL?

YOU MEAN A BOY? NO, NO BOYFRIEND! WHAT ABOUT YOU, MR. BRIAN-- ANY SPECIAL SOMEONE?

I'M SORRY-- I'M NOT USED TO CHAMPAGNE!

IT'S ALL RIGHT, MOXIE. AND I SUPPOSE THERE IS SOMEONE IN NEW YORK...

TONIGHT I'M THE LUCKIEST GIRL IN ALL OF LONDON--OR ANYWHERE!

I ASSURE YOU THE PLEASURE IS ALL MINE.

OH, MR. BRIAN, I CAN'T THANK YOU ENOUGH FOR BRINGING ME!

NONSENSE. YOU ARE ALWAYS BY MY SIDE--I'M THE ONE WHO SHOULD BE THANKING YOU FOR SPENDING SO MUCH TIME WITH ME.

...BUT YOU COULDN'T REALLY CALL THEM A...WELL--

IT'S NONE OF MY BUSINESS, MR. BRIAN. I'M SORRY.

SO COME, LET ME HAVE THIS DANCE.

OH, BUT MY WELFARE HAS ALWAYS BEEN YOUR BUSINESS. FOR WHICH I AM FOREVER IN YOUR DEBT.

I WAS BLUE, JUST AS BLUE AS I COULD BE...

BLUEBIRDS SINGING A SONG.

NOTHING BUT BLUEBIRDS...

BLUE DAYS.

...SKIES WERE GRAY BUT THEY'RE NOT GRAY ANYMORE.

...ALL DAY LONG.

ALL OF THEM GONE.

CENTRAL PARK, NEW YORK CITY.

YOU'VE MADE ME VERY HAPPY BY JOINING ME THIS MORNING.

WHY DO YOU ALWAYS SAY THAT? I'M SURPRISED YOU WANT TO SEE *ME* WHEN YOU'RE IN TOWN.

OH, YOU MAKE ME FEEL ALIVE, DIZZ--AS IF WE HAVE ALL THE JOY, HOPE, AND GLAMOUR IN LIFE AHEAD OF US.

WELL, I FEEL THE SAME WAY ABOUT YOU--SO LET'S ENJOY ALL THE JOY, HOPE, AND GLAMOUR LIFE CAN OFFER!

WELL I'M ONLY REALLY FAMOUS IN BRITAIN.

THAT'S JUST A MATTER OF TIME.

PARDON?

THE BEATLES ARE A POP GROUP-- THEY'LL FADE AWAY, EVENTUALLY. BUT YOU'RE BIG BUSINESS. YOU'LL GO ON FOREVER.

THE BEATLES ARE *NOT* JUST A POP GROUP!!

THAT'S NOT WHAT I MEANT...I MEAN, YOU CAN SEE THAT, BECAUSE YOU HAVE VISION...

MOST PEOPLE SEE JUST A POP GROUP IN THE BEATLES, RIGHT? BUT...

...WHEN I LOOK AT THEM...I SEE BRIAN EPSTEIN. THE SECRET OF THEIR SUCCESS.

GOSH. WELL. THAT'S AWFULLY KIND OF YOU!

87

BUT I MUST SAY THAT IT'S REFRESHING NOT TO BE RECOGNIZED ALWAYS.

LOOK, DIZZ, I WANT TO SHARE SOMETHING WITH YOU. I REALLY ENJOY BEING WITH YOU, AND...

I FEEL PERHAPS YOU'LL UNDERSTAND ME.

WELL, I'LL TRY.

IN ENGLAND, IT'S A SERIOUS CRIME TO...BE THE WAY WE ARE. I'VE NEVER HAD A RELATIONSHIP QUITE LIKE I HAVE WITH YOU.

A RELATIONSHIP?!

BACK HOME IT WOULD BE AGAINST THE LAW! I'D BE THROWN INTO JAIL! I'VE HAD PREVIOUS ENCOUNTERS, BUT THEY'VE ALWAYS NEEDED TO BE IN SECRET, IN DARK AND ROUGH PLACES.

LIKE LATE-NIGHT CENTRAL PARK?

YES, SOMETHING LIKE THAT.

ONCE, MANY YEARS AGO... LIVERPOOL'S A PORT TOWN. AND THERE WAS THIS SAILOR...

IT WAS A DARK STREET, AND I WAS SURE HE WAS INTERESTED IN ME.

SOUNDS... ROMANTIC.

IT WASN'T. I WAS BEATEN, DIZZ. BADLY.

ALL I COULD SEE WAS A HAZE OF RED. I THOUGHT I MIGHT DIE. FOR THE NEXT SEVERAL WEEKS, I LIVED UNDER A KIND OF COLD FEAR. MY LIFE FELT-- SCRIPTED.

AND ALL I COULD DO WAS WAIT NERVOUSLY FOR THE NEXT EPISODE TO BE REVEALED.

I WAS AN EMOTIONAL INVALID, DIZZ-- TOTALLY USELESS, AFRAID TO EVEN SHOW MY FACE IN PUBLIC.

THAT PASSED. AND I DON'T KNOW WHAT HAPPENED TO THE SAILOR. FROM TIME TO TIME, I STILL FEEL THAT COLD, SOLITARY FEAR THAT HE'LL RESURFACE, WHEN I LEAST EXPECT IT...

WHY ARE YOU TELLING ME THIS?

WELL, IT'S LIKE I SAID-- WITH YOU IT'S DIFFERENT. HERE, IN AMERICA, IT'S DIFFERENT!

LOOK, I'M REALLY SORRY THAT HAPPENED TO YOU, BUT THESE THINGS HAPPEN. ALL THE TIME. IT'S NOT A BIG DEAL.

IT'S JUST LIKE...WELL, LIKE A BAD LATE NIGHT HERE IN CENTRAL PARK!

DIZZ--TOGETHER WE HAVE ALL THE THRILL OF THAT DARK AND ROUGH ALLEY, BUT WHEN I'M WITH YOU... I CAN BE *BRIAN*. NOT SOME STRANGER.

IT'S THE FIRST TIME I'VE BEEN ABLE TO...

HAVE YOUR CAKE AND EAT ME, TOO?

BRIAN. I LIKE YOU, BUT PLEASE DON'T EXPECT ME TO SAVE YOU FROM WHATEVER IT IS THAT KEEPS YOU ALONE AT NIGHT.

YOU'VE GOT YOUR PILLS FOR THAT.

EXCUSE ME?!

LET ME GUESS--YOU STARTED TAKING THE PILLS AROUND THE SAME TIME AS THE SAILOR?

I DON'T KNOW WHAT YOU'RE TALKING ABOUT-- OR THAT THAT'S ANY OF YOUR BUSINESS!

OH, BRIAN. DON'T WORRY, YOU'LL SEE ME AROUND. I PROMISE.

YOU SHOULD KEEP CALLING ME WHENEVER YOU'RE IN TOWN. I WANT YOU TO.

THEN WHERE ARE YOU GOING?

TO WORK, OF COURSE.

"HELLO, DADDY! YES, I'M FINE. EVERYONE IS TAKING CARE OF ME..."

AND ALL MY ARTISTES ARE THRIVING! IT'S NOT JUST THE BEATLES ANYMORE.

BILLY J. KRAMER HAS BECOME A HIT IN HIS OWN RIGHT, AND I'VE BOOKED CILLA ON ED SULLIVAN--I'M CONFIDENT SHE'LL BE A BIG STAR IN TELEVISION...

"HA! NO, CILLA WON'T BE BIGGER THAN ELVIS, BUT SHE'LL MAKE HER MARK!"

93

THANKS, DADDY. I LOVE YOU. IS MUM THERE?

HELLO, MUMMY! YES I'M FINE. EVERYONE IS TAKING CARE OF M--

WELL, YES, IN TRUTH, I AM A LITTLE ANXIOUS--

"YOU SEE, I'M TAKING BREAKFAST WITH COLONEL TOM PARKER THIS MORNING, ELVIS PRESLEY'S MANAGER..."

"I ALWAYS DID SAY THAT THE BEATLES WOULD BE BIGGER THAN ELVIS--AND HERE WE ARE!"

IT'S JUST THAT--WELL, I'VE PLANS FOR IT TO BE EVEN BIGGER THAN THIS--AND IT'S ALL HAPPENING SO QUICKLY.

AND IT'S DIFFICULT SOMETIMES. KEEPING IT ALL TOGETHER. WITHOUT A PARTNER...

"WITHOUT SOMEONE TO REALLY RELATE TO, AND SHARE THINGS WITH..."

"EVERYTHING IS TERRIBLY EXCITING-- BUT NO ONE UNDERSTANDS WHAT IT'S LIKE WHEN THE SCREAMS DIE DOWN..."

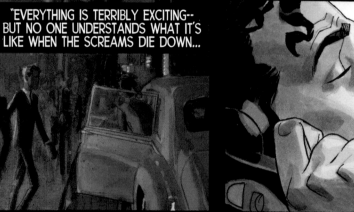

"IT'S SO QUIET... AND LONELY."

SIT DOWN, SON.

ELVIS IS IN HOLLYWOOD RIGHT NOW, FILMING A BIG HOLLYWOOD PITCHA. BUT IF YOU AND YOUR LITTLE BOYS EVER COME BACK TO THE USA, WE SHOULD INTRODUCE THEM TO THE KING.

THEY CAN VISIT US AT GRACELAND, IN MEMPHIS. I HATE NEW YORK. YOU CAN'T TRUST PEOPLE IN THIS TOWN.

THERE ARE JEWS HERE, AND JEWS WILL TAKE ADVANTAGE OF YOU. I WARNED ELVIS THE SAME ABOUT LOS ANGELES-- TOO MANY DAMN JEWS.

A CUT GRAPEFRUIT AND TEA, PLEASE.

I'LL EAT THE BREAKFAST BUFFET.

THAT'S A VERY KIND INVITATION, MR. PARKER.

PLEASE-- CALL ME "THE COLONEL."

THE BEATLES WOULD BE THRILLED TO MEET ELVIS, AS THEY ARE AWFULLY FOND OF HIM.

HE'S THE KING.

INDEED. AND JUST AS MY BOYS ARE EXCITED TO MEET ELVIS, I HAVE VERY MUCH LOOKED FORWARD TO EARNING YOUR FRIENDSHIP.

ONE HUNDRED THOUSAND DOLLARS.

PARDON?

THAT'S WHAT THE FILM STUDIOS PAY ME AS A CONSULTANT ON ELVIS PITCHAS.

FOR ADVICE, ON THE SIDE. AND TO SECURE THE KING. BUT I'LL TALK TO YOU FOR FREE. BECAUSE I LIKE YOU.

WELL...I'M EXTREMELY WORRIED ABOUT SECURITY ON THE BEATLES' UPCOMING WORLD TOUR. IN PLACES LIKE THE PHILIPPINES--

I'VE NEVER HAD PROBLEMS TOURING, AND THE BEATLES AREN'T AS BIG AS ELVIS--SO YOU'VE GOT NOTHING TO WORRY ABOUT. ESPECIALLY IN PLACES LIKE PHILADELPHIA.

THE PHILIPPINES. IN THE FAR EAST.

WELL. ELVIS IS SO POPULAR, WE DON'T NEED TO TOUR THE WORLD.

THAT'S QUITE A...PERPLEXING LUXURY.

BUT SPEAKING OF HOLLYWOOD PICTURES, THERE IS THIS FILM COMPANY I'VE JUST SET UP--

HOW MUCH ARE YOU GONNA GIVE ELVIS TO PLAY THE LEAD?

EXCUSE ME?

WE'LL TAKE ONE MILLION US DOLLARS, NOT A BRITISH PENNY LESS. AND YOU'LL NEED TO SHOOT IN HAWAII OR LAS VEGAS.

FINALLY, YOU'LL NEED ME AS A CONSULTANT TO HELP YOU SECURE ELVIS, WHICH WILL BE AN ADDITIONAL ONE HUNDRED THOUSAND TO ME, AS A SIDE DEAL.

BUT I'LL TALK TO YOU FOR FIFTY THOUSAND. BECAUSE I LIKE YOU. AS I'VE SAID.

I--I JUST WANTED YOUR THOUGHTS ON RETAINING ARTISTIC CONTROL.

HA! NO ONE GIVES A DAMN ABOUT THE MOVIES, EXCEPT MAYBE ELVIS! I HAVEN'T EVEN SEEN THE LAST THREE ELVIS PICTURES.

AS LONG AS THE FEE IS BIG, AND THERE'S ENOUGH SONGS IN IT FOR A RECORD-- ELVIS WILL MAKE MOVIES.

WELL, TO CUT TO THE CHASE, I'M MOST CONCERNED ABOUT KEEPING IT ALL TOGETHER WITH SO MUCH GOING ON FOR THE BEATLES. I WAS WONDERING HOW YOU HANDLE--

--OTHER ARTISTES?

ARTISTES? I HAVE ONE ATTRACTION. ELVIS.

AND I EXPECT THAT MAKES ME BUSIER THAN ALL YOUR PROJECTS COMBINED. THAT'S MY ADVICE TO YOU.

PARDON?

I'VE NO NEED FOR OTHER PROJECTS. ELVIS AND I ARE A PARTNERSHIP. FIFTY-FIFTY...EXCEPT FOR MY SIDE DEALS, OF COURSE, WHICH ARE EXTRA AND NUMEROUS.

YOU TAKE FIFTY PERCENT OF EVERYTHING ELVIS EARNS?!

NO.

ELVIS TAKES FIFTY PERCENT OF EVERYTHING I EARN.

MY CONTRACTS STIPULATE HALF THAT!! AND I'VE FOUND THAT HAVING MULTIPLE SUCCESSFUL ARTISTES PROVES THAT I DIDN'T JUST GET *LUCKY* WITH THE BEATLES.

NOTHING WRONG WITH LUCKY.

AND THE COLONEL HAS NOTHING TO PROVE, SON.

MMMM! DUTCH CHOCOLATE CAKE!

YOU KNOW HIM AS THE MANAGER OF THE BEATLES--

--BUT HE ALSO HANDLES CILLA BLACK, BILLY J. KRAMER AND THE DAKOTAS, AND SO MANY OF TODAY'S TOP STARS. HE'S THE MASTERMIND OF THE SAVILLE THEATRE AND CONCERT HALL, A PUBLISHED AUTHOR, SUCCESSFUL FILM PRODUCER, AND POP PROMOTER!

ACTUALLY, I *DID* JUST GIVE IT A LITTLE CUT.

OH, IT'S NOTHING MUCH. BUT THANK YOU! NOW, YOU'RE INVOLVED IN HEAPS OF EXCITING THINGS IN ADDITION TO THE BEATLES--

--BUT TELL US WHAT YOU ENJOY MOST IN YOUR JET-SETTING LIFE!

VERY STYLISH-- ELEGANT BUT YOUTHFUL-- APPROPRIATE.

WELL, *MALE* BEATLES FANS.

OF COURSE.

SO WHAT WORRIES YOU THE MOST?

WELL...ULTIMATELY I BEAR A CERTAIN STRAIN ALONE...I LIKE TO SEE ONE MAN CLEARLY IN CHARGE, ANSWERABLE FOR HIS OWN MISTAKES. AND THERE ARE PENALTIES TO THAT-- THE CHIEF OF THEM IS LONELINESS.

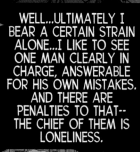

HEAR THAT, GIRLS?! BRITAIN'S BEST-DRESSED MAN AND MOST ELIGIBLE BACHELOR IS A LITTLE LONELY!

 *AND* VOTED BRITAIN'S BEST-DRESSED MAN AND MOST ELIGIBLE BACHELOR UNDER THIRTY! SO LET'S FIND OUT WHAT HE'S REALLY LIKE--BRIAN EPSTEIN!

THANKS FOR JOINING US TODAY, BRIAN! I UNDERSTAND YOU'VE ONLY JUST FLOWN BACK FROM NEW YORK?

INDEED. AND THE PLEASURE IS MINE. IT'S A JOY TO BE BACK IN LONDON--AND TO BE WITH YOU TODAY. HAVE YOU CHANGED YOUR HAIR?

BEST OF ALL AND FAR BEYOND ANYTHING MONEY CAN BUY-- I LOVE TO SIMPLY LEAN ON MY ELBOWS AT THE BACK OF THE CONCERT HALL. WHERE NOBODY NOTICES ME. AND WATCH THE CURTAIN RISE ON MY ARTISTES...

YOU SEE, DEEP DOWN INSIDE, I AM JUST A SIMPLE FAN. AND SO I SIMPLY FEEL EVERYTHING THAT BEATLES FANS FEEL.

 AND I SUPPOSE YOU'VE AN AWFUL LOT OF MONEY TO BE ACCOUNTABLE FOR.

 THE BOYS?

 YES--A SILLY ENDEARMENT, REALLY. AND THE BEATLES CALL ME "EPPY."

NO, NO! NOT WHAT I MEANT AT ALL! I HAVE MANY FRIENDS AND ENJOY A GREAT DEAL OF ENTERTAINMENT AND FUN. I HOPE I'LL NEVER BE LONELY...ALTHOUGH ONE INFLICTS LONELINESS ON ONESELF, TO A CERTAIN EXTENT. AND THAT'S THE DANGER OF HOLDING ONESELF ACCOUNTABLE.

YES, BUT IT ISN'T THE MONEY THAT WORRIES ME...IT'S THE FAILURE. I WON'T TOLERATE FAILURE. AND WHILE THEY DON'T CONCERN THEMSELVES WITH THE BUSINESS, NEITHER DO THE BOYS.

IS RINGO GOING?

TELL US ABOUT PAUL AND JANE!

DOES GEORGE HAVE A STEADY?

IS IS TRUE THAT JOHN'S MARRIED?

WELL, THE PEOPLE HAVE SPOKEN! WHAT CAN YOU DIVULGE?

I THINK BEATLES OUGHT NEVER TO BE MARRIED, BUT THEY WILL BE SOMEDAY-- AND SO, SOMEDAY, I MIGHT BE TOO!

HEAR THAT, GIRLS? BRITAIN'S BEST-DRESSED MAN AND MOST ELIGIBLE BACHELOR MIGHT ONE DAY BE MARRIED! SO SPEAK NOW OR FOREVER HOLD YOUR PEACE!

I'VE GOT AN OBJECTION. ISN'T IT A CRIME IN ENGLAND TO BE GAY?

DON'T YOU BRITS PUT HOMOS IN THE SLAMMER?

HA, HA! THAT'S ONE OF MY AMERICAN FRIENDS WITH THEIR ARRESTING YANKEE HUMOR! SOUNDS STRANGE TO BRITISH EARS, DOESN'T IT?

IT SURE DOES! LET'S TAKE TEN, THEN!

HELLO, BRIAN...

WHAT-- WHAT IS IT YOU WANT THIS TIME?

AREN'T YOU HAPPY TO SEE ME?

HAPPY ?!?

I SPENT EVERY LAST CENT TO GET TO LONDON 'CUZ I'VE MISSED YOU SO BADLY!! I THOUGHT YOU'D BE FLATTERED. CAN'T I STAY WITH YOU?

WHAT?

PLEASE? I'VE REALLY MISSED OUR NIGHTS IN NEW YORK.

LOOK, I DON'T KNOW WHAT THE HELL YOU'RE ON ABOUT...

BUT THIS BUSINESS IS VERY SERIOUS.

DID YOU REALLY MISS ME?

YOU'VE BEEN AWAY SO LONG. AND WHEN YOU'RE IN TOWN YOU DON'T ALWAYS CALL ANYMORE.

SO NOW I WANT TO STAY WITH YOU FOR A FEW DAYS.

PLEASE-- JUST LEAVE.

WE CAN TALK AT MY FLAT LATER. YOU DON'T UNDERSTAND THE SEVERITY OF THE LAWS HERE.

OH I THINK I DO.

AND I ALSO NEED SOME TAXI MONEY.

I HAD TO BORROW A LOT OF CASH TO GET TO LONDON.

COULD I HAVE SOME MONEY TO REPAY MY DEBTS?

FINE-- WHATEVER YOU NEED! PLEASE JUST LEAVE! IMMEDIATELY!

...AND MEET ME AT HOME LATER.

DON'T TREAT ME LIKE A SERVANT! YOU BASTARD!

I LOVED YOU!

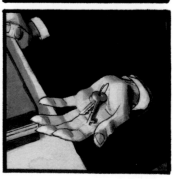

THAT WAS MY WEDDING PLANNER!

NOW WHERE WERE WE? AH, YES, I WAS SAYING THAT YOU'VE NO LACK OF AMBITION. WHAT'S YOUR GREATEST AMBITION IN BUSINESS AND LIFE?

WELL. MY GREATEST AMBITION IN LIFE IS NOT TO MAKE A LOT OF MONEY...

NO, MY GREATEST AMBITION HAS ALWAYS BEEN...TO ACT IN A PLAY.

YES, REGARDLESS OF BOX OFFICE SUCCESS OR POPULAR ACCLAIM.

I'VE ALWAYS WANTED TO SIMPLY BELONG IN A CAST.

WELL--AS SOMEONE ONCE SAID, "ALL THE WORLD'S A STAGE!" SPEAKING OF WHICH, AREN'T THE BEATLES ABOUT TO LAUNCH A RECORD-BREAKING WORLD TOUR?

YES, INDEED. WE'RE GOING TO PLACES LIKE THE PHILIPPINES AND JAPAN BEFORE RETURNING TO THE US.

I'M VERY PROUD TO BE PUTTING THE BOYS IN VENUES THAT POP STARS HAVE NEVER PERFORMED IN BEFORE--SPORTS ARENAS, FOOTBALL STADIUMS, AND THE LIKE.

IT'S A VERY IMPORTANT THING WE'RE ABOUT TO DO.

IMPORTANT?

YES, YOU SEE-- WE'RE ON THE WORLD STAGE NOW. AND THERE'S A RESPONSIBILITY TO THAT.

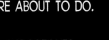

I BELIEVE WE ARE ALL IN THIS TOGETHER--PUBLIC, ARTISTES, MANAGEMENT, PRESS, THE ENTIRE ENTERTAINMENT INDUSTRY...

...AND I BELIEVE WE SHOULD ALL BE IDENTIFIED WITH **THE GREAT CAUSE**...

...OF CHEERING US ALL UP.

I'M SORRY, FATHER. IT SEEMS THE BEATLES ARE MORE POPULAR THAN JESUS NOW. I DON'T KNOW WHICH WILL GO FIRST--ROCK AND ROLL OR CHRISTIANITY.

ROAR!

OUR HERO!

MR. BRIAN SAVES THE DAY AGAIN!

THE MAGAZINE EVERYBODY'S TALKING ABOUT!

DATEbook

29 JULY 1966

"Lennon Claims Beatles Bigger Than Jesus Christ!"

TELL THEM TO GET STUFFED! I'VE GOT NOTHING TO APOLOGIZE FOR!

Part III: If Love Were All

DON'T BE RIDICULOUS. THIS IS THE HOUR WHEN YOU WILL BREAK YOUR GOLDEN RULE AGAINST APOLOGIZING.

I'M THE LEADER OF THIS GROUP, AND I CALL THE SHOTS! CANCEL THE AMERICAN TOUR-- I'D RATHER THAT THAN HAVE TO GET UP AND LIE!

THE LEADER? THE TOUR? IS THAT WHAT YOU THINK THIS IS ALL ABOUT?

THEN LET ME BREAK MY OWN GOLDEN RULE AGAINST SHARING MY CONCERNS...

I AM SERIOUSLY AFRAID THAT YOU AND THE BOYS WILL BE *ASSASSINATED* IN AMERICA.

ASSASSINATED?

JOHN, THE SITUATION HERE IS FAR WORSE THAN IT WAS IN THE PHILIPPINES.

THE PHILIPPINES?! *THE PHILIPPINES?!?!*

THE PHILIPPINES WAS A LAUGH, WASN'T IT?

YOU DID AT THAT!

JOHN! THIS IS HARDLY THE TIME FOR LAUGHTER! AND I BROKE OUT INTO HIVES AFTER THAT EXPERIENCE!

LOOK-- SERIOUSLY. IT WOULD BREAK MY HEART IF THE BEATLES STOPPED TOURING. AND I'M STILL PREPARED TO CANCEL THE TOUR. BUT IT'S NOT ABOUT THAT.

ASSASSINATED.

POP

WELL IT LOOKS LIKE YOU'RE FINISHED, BRIAN.

OR MAYBE NOT YET. THERE'S ONE PIECE OF BAGGAGE LEFT...YOUR BRIEFCASE.

OH, IT'S SAFE.

AND SAFELY INSIDE THAT LITTLE BRIEFCASE ARE YOUR FUCKING DRUGS, YOUR QUEER LITTLE LOVE NOTES, ALL YOUR LIES AND BULLSHIT...AND GUESS WHAT ELSE IS IN THERE?

I'VE GOT YOUR *DICK* INSIDE THAT BRIEFCASE. AND I'M GOING TO SHOW ITS UGLY, PATCHY, SHIT-SMEARED, CIRCUMCISED FAGGOT HEAD TO THE WHOLE WORLD...

UNLESS WE WORK SOMETHING OUT. FINAL. AND FINANCIAL.

I WILL PAY YOU WHATEVER YOU WANT.

BUT IF BRIAN EVER SEES YOU AGAIN--

--I WILL KILL YOU MYSELF.

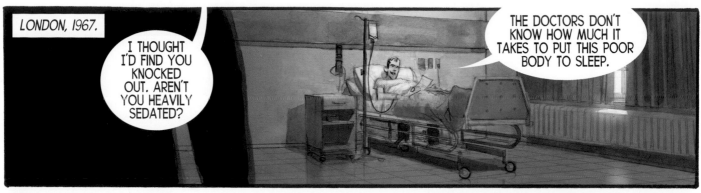

LONDON, 1967.

I THOUGHT I'D FIND YOU KNOCKED OUT. AREN'T YOU HEAVILY SEDATED?

THE DOCTORS DON'T KNOW HOW MUCH IT TAKES TO PUT THIS POOR BODY TO SLEEP.

IT'S GOOD OF YOU TO COME. LAST YEAR TOOK ITS TOLL...HAVE YOU HEARD FROM DIZZ?

YOU WON'T BE SEEING HIM AGAIN. YOU SHOULD BE RESTING.

REST? MY MANAGEMENT CONTRACT WITH THE BOYS IS SET TO EXPIRE SHORTLY... YOU KNOW I DON'T BELIEVE THEY WOULD WANT TO BE MANAGED BY ANYONE ELSE-- THOUGH I SUPPOSE YOU'D NEED TO ASK THEM TO BE SURE.

BRIAN, PLEASE--

WELL REGARDLESS, I'M WORKING ON OUR NEXT BIG THING. THIS RECORD THEY'RE COMPOSING-- IT'S GOING TO PROVE ONCE AND FOR ALL THAT POP MUSIC IS AN ART FORM! YOU KNOW I'VE BEEN SAYING IT FOR YEARS.

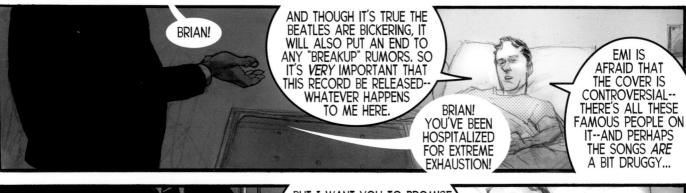

BRIAN!

AND THOUGH IT'S TRUE THE BEATLES ARE BICKERING, IT WILL ALSO PUT AN END TO ANY "BREAKUP" RUMORS. SO IT'S *VERY* IMPORTANT THAT THIS RECORD BE RELEASED-- WHATEVER HAPPENS TO ME HERE.

BRIAN! YOU'VE BEEN HOSPITALIZED FOR EXTREME EXHAUSTION!

EMI IS AFRAID THAT THE COVER IS CONTROVERSIAL-- THERE'S ALL THESE FAMOUS PEOPLE ON IT--AND PERHAPS THE SONGS *ARE* A BIT DRUGGY...

...BUT I WANT YOU TO PROMISE ME IT WILL BE RELEASED *EXACTLY* AS THE BOYS ENVISION--LET EMI WRAP IT IN PAPER BAGS, IF THEY MUST.

BRIAN! THAT'S ENOUGH! YOU NEED TO REST!!

BROWN BAGS FOR SERGEANT PEPPER'S!

FINE! I PROMISE. NOW PLEASE--*REST.*

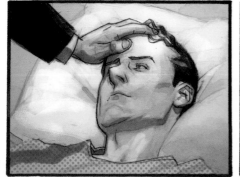

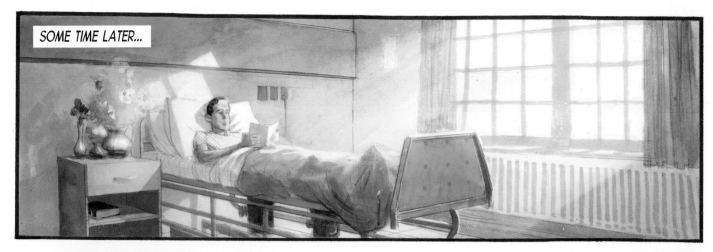

SOME TIME LATER...

"I'M SORRY WE HAVEN'T BEEN ROUND MORE THESE PAST FEW MONTHS, BUT YOU KNOW I LOVE YOU, EPPY, I REALLY DO. —JOHN"

EPPY! IT'S DONE! AND IT'S PERFECT.

IT'S NOT PERFECT AT ALL. BUT IT IS BRILLIANT.

NONSENSE. IT'S PERFECT.

WHATEVER YOU SAY, SIR PAUL.

ENOUGH! KNOWING YOU TWO, IT'S BOTH PERFECT AND BRILLIANT. AND IT CALLS FOR CELEBRATION. WE MUST THROW A PRESS EVENT AND A RELEASE PARTY IMMEDIATELY!

NOT AT ALL. WE WERE TALKING ABOUT THE BEATLES-- WHAT ELSE?

THEY'VE OFFICIALLY QUIT TOURING, AND I HEARD JOHN AND PAUL GET ON EACH OTHER'S NERVES. I RECKON THEY'RE BREAKING UP.

MAYBE THAT'S WHY NOBODY SEES HIM ANYMORE. I HEAR EVEN ANDREW OLDHAM CAN'T GET A MEETING!

WELL IF THIS IS A FAREWELL EVENT, I SUPPOSE WE OUGHT TO BE LOOKING OUT FOR THE "NEXT BEATLES."

WHAT'S HE THAT WISHES SO?

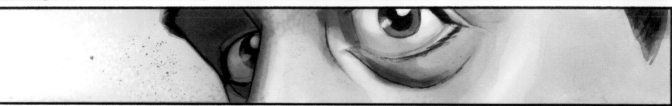

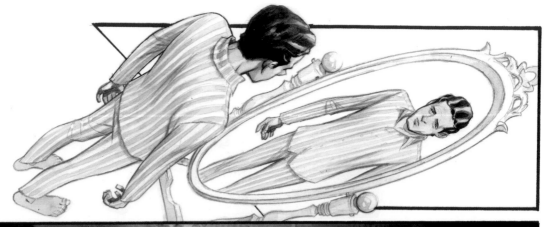

FOUR!

THREE!

TWO!

ONE!

ACTION!

"I BELIEVE IN DOING WHAT I CAN, IN CRYING WHEN I MUST...

"...IN LAUGHING WHEN I CHOOSE.

"IF LOVE WERE ALL, I SHOULD BE LONELY.

"I BELIEVE THE MORE YOU LOVE A MAN, THE MORE YOU PLACE YOUR TRUST...

"...THE MORE YOU'RE BOUND TO LOSE.

"ALTHOUGH, WHEN SHADOWS FALL, I THINK IF ONLY...

"...SOMEBODY SPLENDID REALLY NEEDED ME...

"SOMEONE AFFECTIONATE AND DEAR. CARES WOULD BE ENDED IF I KNEW THAT HE...

"...WANTED TO HAVE ME NEAR.

"BUT I BELIEVE THAT SINCE MY LIFE BEGAN, THE MOST I'VE HAD IS JUST...

"...A TALENT TO AMUSE...

"OH--IF LOVE WERE ALL..."

HELLO, MR. BRIAN. I NOTICED YOU LEFT. I'M GLAD YOU'RE RESTING... YOU DESERVE TO, YOU KNOW.

I CAN'T SLEEP.

I'M WORRIED ABOUT THE FUTURE, MOXIE. I'M WORRIED THAT IT'S CIRCULAR, AND EVERY STORY WILL REPEAT EVENTUALLY.

SO WHILE IT'S TRUE THAT I'VE ACCOMPLISHED SO MANY THINGS, THAT I MAY HAVE EVEN BUILT A BETTER TOMORROW...

I STILL DON'T KNOW HOW MY *STORY* ENDS...

I DON'T KNOW HOW IT WILL REPEAT.

I'M AFRAID I DON'T UNDERSTAND.

I WANT A HAPPY ENDING! SO I WILL KEEP TRYING, KEEP PUSHING MYSELF TOWARD WHAT-EVER IT TAKES-- UNTIL I FIGURE OUT HOW TO GET IT!

AND IF I NEED TO, I'LL FIGURE OUT HOW TO GET ANOTHER CHANCE, EVEN AFTER THE STORY ENDS.

I WANT TO BREAK THE CIRCLE!

WELL, IF TIME IS CIRCULAR AND OUR STORIES HAVE ALREADY BEEN TOLD...

MAYBE WE CAN'T CHANGE THE ENDING?

MAYBE WE SHOULDN'T BE TRYING.

MAYBE THE BEST THING-- WOULD BE TO JUST GET SOME REST...

YES.

THANK YOU, MOXIE. YOU'RE RIGHT OF COURSE--

I NEED SOME REST.

WHERE'S JOHN? I NEED TO SEE JOHN!

JOHN!

JOHN?

OH. PAUL.

I'M SORRY, EPPY-- JOHN COULDN'T COME. HE'S BEEN...BUSY.

YOU KNOW, WITH, UM, CYNTHIA.

AND OTHER... THINGS.

BUSY.

WELL, HE WOULD HAVE COME, I THINK. BUT HE'S IN BANGOR, WITH THE MAHARISHI, WHO SAYS...

"EVERYTHING WILL BE LOST IF THE MEDITATIVE CIRCLE IS BROKEN!"

BUT YOU'RE THERE, TOO. AND STILL YOU CAME.

YES. I CAME. I HEARD YOU CALLING. SO I CAME. WHAT ELSE COULD I DO?

BUT I'VE COME FOR ALL OF US!

YOU SEE, WHEN YOU GET RIGHT DOWN TO IT, WE'RE JUST FOUR SCOUSERS WHO LOVE YOU...

AND THAT'S WHAT IT'S ALL ABOUT. LOVE. FOR ME, ANYWAY.

LOVE?

"LOVE ME DO"...? "CAN'T BUY ME LOVE"...? "LOVELY RITA"...? "SHE LOVES YOU, YEAH YEAH YEAH"...?

EPPY--WITH YOUR HELP, I RECKON WE'VE BROUGHT LOTS OF LOVE INTO THE WORLD.

I'M AWFULLY PROUD OF THAT. AREN'T YOU?

LOVE...

LOOK, I KNOW YOU WANTED TO SEE JOHN, BUT THE TRUTH IS HE COULDN'T BE BOTHERED TO EVEN NOTICE WHAT'S GOING ON!

PAUL. YOU'RE IN CHARGE OF MY LEGACY. I HAVE ALWAYS FELT THAT WAY ABOUT YOU.

WHAT?!

I'M GLAD YOU CAME. I'M PROUD YOU CAME. YOU PUT IT IN A WAY I NEVER COULD--JOHN WON'T BE BOTHERED...

...AND YOU'VE ALWAYS BEEN MORE SAVVY, PAYING ATTENTION TO THE DETAILS AND SO FORTH.

BUT REMEMBER THIS ABOVE ALL--NOTHING IS MORE IMPORTANT THAN FAMILY. THE BEATLES ARE A *FAMILY*.

SO YOU MUST STAY TOGETHER AT ALL COSTS.

EPPY, I DON'T KNOW IF I CAN HANDLE THAT.

I DON'T KNOW THAT I'LL ALWAYS WANT THAT!

YOU CAN'T. YOU WON'T. AND STILL I LEAVE YOU NO CHOICE.

WAIT! EPPY!!

HOW?

NAT! I'M SO GLAD YOU'VE COME. I HAVE SOMETHING EXTREMELY IMPORTANT TO TELL YOU.

HELLO, BRIAN. TELL ME.

I'VE FIGURED IT OUT. ABOUT MOXIE.

MOXIE?

SHE'S NOT HUMAN, NAT. SHE'S SOME KIND OF SPIRIT--MAYBE THE INCARNATION OF *AMBITION* OR SOME SUCH.

MOXIE, GET IT? BUT WHAT I HAVEN'T SUSSED OUT IS IF SHE'S AN ANGEL OR A DEMON--OR BOTH.

BRIAN, WHAT THE HELL ARE YOU TALKING ABOUT?

EITHER WAY, I'M GRATE-FUL FOR HER. SHE'S BEEN AN INVALUABLE ASSISTANT, AND SHE INTRODUCED ME TO THE BEATLES... AND SHE'S *LOVED* ME.

BRIAN. I HAVE NO CLUE WHAT YOU'RE TALKING ABOUT.

AH. I SEE.

WHAT I DO KNOW IS THAT YOU CAN REST EASY NOW...I'VE GOT SOME GOOD NEWS.

THE MERCHANDISING ISSUES HAVE BEEN LEGALLY SETTLED, AT LONG LAST.

SO REST. YOU'VE GOT A BIG REHEARSAL TOMORROW. AND YOU'LL NEED TO GIVE THE PERFORMANCE OF YOUR LIFE.

HELLO, MR. BRIAN. I NOTICED YOU LEFT. I'M GLAD YOU'RE RESTING... YOU DESERVE TO, YOU KNOW.

I OFTEN WONDER IF HE WAS RIGHT ABOUT ME...

YES, MOXIE. I'M RESTING.

MOXIE, YOU'VE DONE SO MUCH FOR ME SINCE THIS ALL BEGAN, AT NEMS, JUST SIX YEARS AGO.

AND NOW I NEED YOUR HELP MORE THAN EVER-- I'M FINALLY GOING TO START LOOKING AFTER MYSELF.

THAT'S WONDERFUL, MR. BRIAN!

...AND WHEN DID IT BECOME TOO LATE?

WHEN DID WE CROSS THE POINT OF NO RETURN?

I'M GOING TO PUT ALL MY BUSINESSES ON HOLD. BECAUSE, YOU SEE, I'VE JUST HAD THE HAPPIEST NEWS OF MY LIFE...

I'VE PASSED AN AUDITION...I'M GOING TO BE IN A PLAY!

WILL YOU PLEASE MAKE THE NECESSARY ARRANGE-MENTS?

AND WOULD I EVER FORGIVE MYSELF?

NEVER.

OF COURSE, MR. BRIAN. IT WOULD BE MY PLEASURE. IT'S JUST...I DON'T KNOW WHAT HAPPENS TOMORROW.

YES, IT'S TOMORROW THAT'S THE CARDINAL PROBLEM.

BUT WHATEVER HAPPENS TOMORROW, MOXIE, ONE THING IS CERTAIN...

...IT MUST NOT BE ALLOWED TO LOOK AFTER ITSELF.

NEVER.

132

AND IN THE END...

BRIAN EPSTEIN ACCOMPLISHED MORE BY THE AGE OF THIRTY-TWO THAN MOST PEOPLE DO IN AN ENTIRE LIFETIME.

BUT, OH--IF LOVE WERE ALL...

...THE WORLD IS A RICHER PLACE FOR LOVE.

...I SHOULD BE LONELY.

Within two years, the Beatles would disband in a very public sea

of personal acrimony and professional lawsuits. Nevertheless, the

legacy that Brian orchestrated and protected would insure that the

Beatles remained among the best-loved and most inspirational

artists—in any artistic discipline—for all time. Their message

of Love would continue to burn brightly, even as the fire died.

"If anyone was the Fifth Beatle, it was Brian."

—Paul McCartney, 1999

THIS FEELIN' THAT REMAINS . . .

Afterword by Vivek J. Tiwary

"Mythology is better and more fondly remembered than history! So we create legends rather than recount truths."

The Fifth Beatle is a true labor of love. Telling the Brian Epstein story has been my "life's work"—as strange as it is to use that phrase, since I hope to have many more years ahead of me. But I've had an ongoing and unrequited love affair with the Brian Epstein story for more than half my life.

As romantic as that may sound, my fascination with Brian Epstein started with my head rather than my heart. I found my way to his story when I was a student at the Wharton School of Business, dreaming of working in entertainment and managing bands, hungry for professional inspiration. My mother, Nandini Beharry Tiwary, always taught me not only to work hard in the present—but to study the past, find inspiration wherever you can, and carve your own future. She also filled my childhood home with the sounds of classical music . . . and the Beatles.

I was stunned to discover how little information there is available about Brian Epstein and the management of the Beatles, and so I dove deeply into intense research that has literally gone on for over two decades. Over those years I've had the good fortune of breaking bread with a number of people who were important to Brian—from artists he managed, to coworkers, to members of the Epstein family, to those few people who he considered close friends. In truth, some were reluctant to speak with me at first. But I did my best to convey my genuine interest and passion for Brian's legacy, and in the end each and every one of these fascinating folks proved warm and welcoming, freely sharing their memories (and in some cases, their memorabilia) about Brian.

The business student in me was of course richly rewarded with the "case study" I uncovered in Brian Epstein . . . But it was the human, emotional side of Brian's story that deeply resonated with me. Brian was an outsider in his chosen field—and I have often felt that way myself, as a first-generation American of Indian origin, wading my way through the changing tides of the film, television, and theater industries. Brian Epstein became my "historical mentor." He's a person whose history I've sought to learn from—both what to do and what *not* to do. Brian was a flawed and imperfect hero, but he was a hero all the same . . . *So like all worthy heroes, why shouldn't Brian Epstein have a life in comics?*

Now if I'm such an Epstein expert, Beatles historians might rightly question some points of history in *The Fifth Beatle*. Were the Beatles playing a gig in Taunton when John Lennon found out Cynthia was pregnant? Where is Pete Best in all of this? Did Ed Sullivan really negotiate with Brian using a ventriloquist's dummy? (Believe it or not, *that* actually happened.*) And who—or what—the hell is Moxie?

If *The Fifth Beatle* were a film, we might include an end credit like "This story is based on actual events. In certain cases incidents, characters, and timelines have been changed for dramatic purposes." But that disclaimer reads more like a legal attempt to cover one's ass than a heartfelt attempt to capture the essence of a man.

As it turns out, almost everything in the pages you've just read actually *did* happen. But conveying the truth—while important—has never been my primary goal. My goal with *The Fifth Beatle* is to use 130 pages of my words and Andrew C. Robinson's gorgeous art to reveal not just the facts but the *poetry* behind the Brian Epstein story. His is a painfully human story about the struggle to overcome seemingly insurmountable odds. A story about staggering ambition yielding staggering success. A story about wanting too much, too soon, while not focusing on the things that really matter. A story about being an outsider, and trying desperately to belong. A story of triumph and tragedy. A story full of dreams, hope, and music . . .

A story that changed my life.

I hope it will inspire yours, in some small but meaningful way. In which case, *The Fifth Beatle* will have been a life's work done well.

—VIVEK J. TIWARY
New York, 2013

THE FREEDOM TO MARRY

"I think Beatles ought never to be married, but they will be someday—and someday, I might be too . . ."

—Brian Epstein, 1964

In 1964, while Brian Epstein was engaged in bringing the most exhilaratingly liberating pop phenomenon in history to America's shores, I was a college student in Alabama, warily taking stock of how my gayness might affect my prospects in life.

Both Brian and I, in our separate worlds, knew that we were automatic felons in the eyes of the law. Forget about being allowed to marry another man someday! I just hoped I could stay out of jail.

Epstein's dream of enabling the Beatles to become "bigger than Elvis" was audacious. It was modest, though, compared to what actually transpired. As we know now, the "Fab Four" from Liverpool were destined to both ride and help fuel the international tidal wave of exuberant social change that we call The Sixties.

I am no longer an automatic criminal, and if Brian were alive today, he wouldn't be, either. Beatles songs didn't make that happen, but their spirit helped make an unending expansion of human possibilities feel joyous instead of scary.

Indeed, far from trying to market my cartoons from behind bars, I am legally married today to a man whom I've loved for thirty-four years. Many heroes and liberationist organizations have played a part in making this possible, but in light of the most recent court battles won, it seems appropriate to single out one in particular. That's what the creators of *The Fifth Beatle* have done by forging a spiritual and economic alliance with Freedom to Marry. I've been invited to add these words to their endorsement because of the role that advocacy organization has played in enriching my own life.

There's more to be done. In thirty-seven states, lesbians and gay men remain deprived of their full rights of citizenship. "All You Need Is Love," that thrilling Beatles lyric, may be over-simplified as a rule of life, but all of us do need love an awful lot! Hopefully, remembering the Beatles' music and contemplating the energy one gay man put into helping them enlarge the world's view of love's potential will encourage readers of *The Fifth Beatle* to contribute what they can to Freedom to Marry so the good work can go on.

—HOWARD CRUSE
Williamstown, July 2013

Freedom to Marry is the campaign to win marriage nationwide. By working to win the freedom to marry in more states, grow the national majority for marriage, and end federal marriage discrimination, Freedom to Marry is creating the climate for another Supreme Court victory, one that will secure the freedom to marry throughout the country, in a matter of years, not decades. Learn more by visiting them at **www.freedomtomarry.org**.

FREEDOM
TO MARRY

VIVEK J. TIWARY

Vivek's earliest childhood memories include browsing the comic-book racks at Forbidden Planet with his parents and listening to their Beatles records at home. He would grow up to be an award-winning producer of theater, film, and television with productions including Green Day's *American Idiot*, *The Addams Family*, and *A Raisin in the Sun*, among others. *The Fifth Beatle: The Brian Epstein Story* is his first book, and he is currently writing the screenplay for its film adaptation. He lives in New York City with his inspiring wife, Tracy, their two delightful children, Kavi and Nandini, and a feisty papillon named Sukhi. Visit him at TiwaryEnt.com.

ANDREW C. ROBINSON

Growing up on the family farm in Florida, Andrew C. Robinson was quite the daydreamer, with a huge fascination for artists like Frank Frazetta, Walt Simonson, and his influential older brother Roby. Before graduating from the Savannah College of Art and Design, Andrew landed his first professional comic-book job. His career began illustrating short stories for *Dark Horse Presents*. Since then, he has seen his paintings published by all major comic-book publishers in the industry, contributing beautifully illustrated covers for such titles as *King Conan*, *Detective Comics* (Batman), *Hawkman*, *Starman*, *Action Comics* (Superman), *Iron Man*, *X-Man*, and *Justice Society of America*. Andrew is also a writer and a creator, currently working on his own creation—*Dusty Star*. Andrew lives in Altadena, California, with his lovely Leah and their daughter Ella. To learn more about his art and projects, visit NextExitComics.com.

KYLE BAKER

Kyle Baker grew up a fan of the old Beatles cartoons, and the Beatles were his first favorite band. As a toddler, he could often be found singing "Ob-La-Di, Ob-La-Da" and "The Continuing Story of Bungalow Bill." Today, Kyle is an award-winning cartoonist, comic book writer/artist, and animator known for his graphic novels (including *Why I Hate Saturn* and *Nat Turner*) and for a 2000s revival of the classic series *Plastic Man*. He has won numerous Eisner Awards and Harvey Awards for his work in the comics field, and has worked for such companies as Disney, Warner Bros. Feature Animation, HBO, DreamWorks, Cartoon Network, Marvel Comics, DC Entertainment, Saatchi & Saatchi, Watson-Guptill, RCA/BMG, Random House, *Nickelodeon Magazine*, *Rugrats*, Scholastic, *Goosebumps*, and others.